The Noctilucent Cloud
AND OTHER MEMORIES

Reba Owen

To order additional copies of this book, contact:
Xlibris
844-714-8691
www.Xlibris.com
Orders@Xlibris.com

ISBN: Softcover   979-8-3694-1139-1
        EBook   979-8-3694-1138-4

Library of Congress Control Number: 2023921894

Print information available on the last page

Rev. date: 11/17/2023

Dedicated to my Brother and Sister

Dudley Nelson and Cookie Erlingheuser

"I can ripple the moon and scatter the stars on the surface of the lake, duet the owl and the nighthawk, but I am helpless to ever find you again." 10/ 2023

Noctilucent Cloud

A glowing aura when light is gone
and sparrows have ceased their vespers.
Suspended above the harbor as if
to guide lost ships and landlocked men
to safety.
Some say not a sign of anything,
just ice crystals in the atmosphere.
The ancients who sky watched didn't mention them until
others who came later said these clouds escaped the Earth's heart,
through Krakatoa's mouth.

Reminiscing

What is it about the autumn that makes us reminisce?
About maples when the sun sets, full moon rising in the firs,
you building a driftwood fire at the first chill of evening
with those hands I loved to touch.
Suddenly I am young again, and you are not even on my path yet.
The pumpkins are ready. I get carameled apples for my birthday.
My mom chooses whether the Jack 'O Lantern will be frowning or smiling.
We are all deciding what to be on Halloween, and if Mr. Wenger
will again dress as Wolf Man, and jump out of the bamboo to
momentarily terrify us.
Now there is little time left for remembering. No way to know how
many more autumns there will be. But until that time I will find comfort
in the thickening air, in the V's of geese, the phosphorescent surf, and
the memory of that driftwood fire and your hands.

Reba Owen
08/26/2021

*A*n Acrostic Poem

High above the skeleton trees
A broom soars the night breeze.
Live bats scatter high and low.
Lanterns of carved pumpkins glow.
Over fields of yellow corn,
Witches fly till light of morn.
Evil spirits
Evil spirits hiding near
No one is safe when they are here.

10/31/2023

"Safe"

The Imagining

One night I imagined sitting on the cusp of the new moon
and watching the new year approaching
the Earth below.
From that height there is no destruction, no hatred,
no disease, no tears.
Just the sweet salt of the oceans,
the resins of the forests,
and the new year humming, ringing, strumming
a bel canto of hope.

Reba Owen c 2018

The 10.2 Tide

Today is a 10 foot tide, pushed from a hazy moon,
to the sea. I am here to watch as logs of cedar and alder,
cottonwood and spruce, smash about, where last year a child
was ripped from his father's grasp, and lost to the foam forever.
Where sneaker waves carve away the coastline and stony berm.
Where my house tilts even more toward the horizon, days numbered,
as are my days.
The years of sunlight, of picnics, cards and castles, of pancakes and salal
jelly, driftwood coals, crab catching, crowned sparrows, turn stones, and
oyster catchers, south wind rain, and my riding a smooth green wave...
all are drowning in the roar of the surf below.

"The Last Portal
Picture at the Cabin"

The Doctoral Dissertation

The Diagnostic Manual of Mental Disorders says "Patients with animal phobias are 75% to 90% female. Rosy, a phlebotomist, told me as my blood bubbled into a syringe, that more men than women topple from the lab's stools and crash, unconscious to the floor.

If a parade of snakes, spiders, and mice filed through the lab, there could be piles of women passed out on the shiny floor or perched screaming atop the lab counters. If birds and large moths fluttered through the hospital, the women might trample each other to get out the door.

I have always puzzled over other humans' fears of the natural world. Snakes and spiders can bite, Those phobias are plausible. In writing my dissertation, I asked people how often they have been attacked by a snake, mouse or spider. The most common answer was "not often" or "never". A question like "how many chickadees and moths have rearranged your hair or tried to rip off your eye brows?" would get a quick answer. "Don't be silly." But a few phobic individuals would swear, "these animals will strike if given a chance. Most likely they would attack us while we were most vulnerable.... Like when we were standing on a window ledge at night, forty feet above the raging surf and rocks during a wind storm!"

Such statements and feelings are irrational. Moths may fly in your face as they head to your closet full of wool and cashmere. Snakes prefer to bite slugs and insects. They lay sunning in your path to warm their blood, not to scare the bejeebers out of you. Spiders prefer insect blood to humans' unless you happen to roll over on their side of the bed. Few mice in the U.S. have run out from under couches and clamped their teeth permanently into someone's calf muscle.

Certainly a chickadee or chicken flying around the kitchen could dislodge a horrible childhood memory of some killer parakeet. Teeth and phobias are interlocked. Take my sister for example: she is deathly afraid of moths. I often ask her, "why are you so afraid of moths and not butterflies?" "Because moths are fuzzy and have big sharp teeth. They fly around in the dark until they find your jugular."

"Have you ever been attacked?" I persisted

"Yes, yes many times! Remember when we were playing poker six years ago and that moth flew out of the curtains and got Mom and I?"

"Of course I remember that game. You and Mom weren't 'gotten'. You and Mom crushed the moth when you knocked the card table over. Dad was mad because he had a straight flush."

Mothpokerphobia could be added to the other 275 known phobias. Bats are on that list. "Vespertiliophobic". Now the Greek and Latin are gone, replaced by "Panic Attack" or "Anxiety Disorder". Treatment is now a pill. In the old days, treatment took 2 routes. "Flooding" meant the patient was thrown into a dark smelly bat cave with it's thousands of squeaking denizens. "Desensitization" was the slow process of showing the sufferer cute pictures of bats, videos and stories until the patient could hold a live vampire bat in their hand.

After completing my Doctoral Dissertation research, I am still puzzled how anyone can have a phobia to animals. Especially ones that are small enough to swat or stomp on. My work and Dissertation were not considered serious enough by the University PHD Committee. I immediately developed a phobia of formalized education. I left the school forever. I returned home to see if that blue tailed skink was still hanging around the larkspurs..... waiting to bite somebody

Rat

When I was young collecting "critters" was an activity of mine that didn't always sit well with the adults around me. Snakes, salamanders, frogs, and one time, even a baby (teen) rat. I kept it secured in the garage in a box. It was a Norway or wharf rat, that had the potential to chew up a house. One night it escaped and disappeared. Years later, being suspicious, I asked my parents if they knew what happened to that rat. They told me they couldn't bring themselves to kill it, so they put it on a plank and floated it down the Willamette River in front of our house.

$\mathcal{R}$it Resurection

Hued eggs, chocolate and caramel
white rabbits proliferating
as is their course.
Chinese pastel baskets full
of glittering plastic grass,
Sunrisers eating sweet crosses
of glazed pastries.
The dogwood is blooming and weeping.
Stigmata appear on palms and ankles,
dripping blood.
The sepulchre lies empty
And the lie goes on and on.

3/31/2010

Nik and Bernie Meme

Idioms and sayings

Idioms are groups of words which together can change the meanings of the individual words. I began thinking about the history of idioms in my family. Starting with a little rhyme of my grandmother Reba who was born in the late 1800's. "Whistling girls and cackling hens, both will come to no good end." But the main source of idioms and sayings came from my "gumshoe" father. Gumshoe was the name given to detectives whose soft soles allowed them to sneak up on crooks. My father was a Portland policeman long before anyone knew about political correctness: Needless to say his language was often colorful: to describe personality he might say: "worthless as tits on a boar," "not the sharpest knife in the drawer," "dead as a door nail," "dumb as a stump," "happy as a clam," cool as a cucumber, crazy as a coot. A pretty woman passing by would get: "Look at the ears on that rabbit!" "He's a space cadet". "She going round the bend". Smart as a fox.

My dad had been a Navy man so many saying were nautical. "Batten down the hatches." "We will Jerry rig that". (he mixed jury rig and jerry built) "Red sky at night, sailors delight, red sky at morning sailors warning." White caps meant "the sheep are out". Down wind and up wind (in relation to smells)

My dad loved the beach but my mom not so much because of the rain and north wind. Dad would always so "Jo look there's a blue line on the horizon!" Or kids "look there's enough blue sky for a Dutchman's britches" These weather descriptions are probably why my mom was often "three sheets to the wind".

He would put down other people's jokes telling by saying "Columbus kicked the slats out of his cradle when he heard that joke."

Two of my favorite inherited sayings are "I was born at night but not last night. And something bad "would gag a maggot".

My grand daughter lives and works in LA and has been teaching me how to talk the language there so I won't appear as a country bumpkin when I visit. If you want to know how many people are at a party or event you ask: "How deep we rollin" and end with "Slime" which means friend. Remember at the height of covid when they were limiting the number of customers at a store? In LA you could say "How deep we rollin Slime? No Problem. But not something you want to throw out here at Safeway or Costco.....

And lastly I don't say this out loud but I do think it. It can refer to women and men apparently: Put your big girl panties on.

Mrs. Kreitler's Opus

"The worms crawl out
the worms crawl in,
the worms play pinochle on your chin."

That song would turn Mrs. Kreitler's face as red as her hair. Mrs. Kreitler was our grade school music teacher. She had definite ideas as to what was acceptable music. My formal music education began and ended in her class. Hours of tracing treble clefs never produced an inkling of understanding or caring for their importance in the world. Yet, Mrs. Kreitler caused "The Bells of St. Marys" to ring poignantly in my brain forever...."the young loves, the true loves"; or the "Roses of Picardy", which I now know was a popular 1916 song associated with the horrifying trench warfare in WW1

The Girl Scouts of America contributed greatly to a less formal part of my musical appreciation. A clip's ringing on a flag pole in the evening breeze can transport me back to taps at the edge of a froggy lake. Long before I was able to cross the great oceans, other lands beckoned: "It's the Far Northland that's a calling me home...." "I must arise now and go to Innesfree." I knew the high and low parts to "The Ashgrove" long before I knew of Wales. Before there was a modern Israel we danced and sang to "Hava Nagila".

There are no better rock 'n roll credentials than to have been a teenager in the Fifties. "A Whole Lotta Shakin" was going on after Bill Haley and his Comets started with "Rock Around the Clock." Ed Sullivan cut Elvis off at the waist when the King of Rock 'roll first appeared on TV. Elvis's hips were the most scandalous activity anyone had ever seen. Kids loved it and so did their moms. Can I remember anything about 1956? Not one memory comes forth except that day in the Milwaukie High lunch room when "Heartbreak Hotel" caused 200 teenagers to go silent in rapt attention.

Because of trying to maintain my GPA, I missed the Sixties completely. Radios were not permitted in the college library where I spent most of my time. Cell phones were unheard of. The drugs, war protests, long hair, and free sex, all passed me by unnoticed. Folk songs revived, but I already knew "Shenandoah", "The Patriot Game", "Riding on the City of New Orleans". I also knew the war was lost because even Genghis Khan had been unable to defeat the Vietnamese.

The ukulele advanced my repertoire of songs. Songs from my parent's forty-five records came forth like moonlight in the night: "Blue Moon", "Moon of Monacurra", "Moonlight in Vermont". "Moonlight Becomes You". I learned that hundreds of songs could be played with just three chords. E A and B7 would give you almost any rock 'n roll, blues or boogie woogie tune. Some guitar lessons opened doors to timing, beat, and pitch which I promptly forgot and which I still find troublesome.

Classical music was always a foreign language to me. Then the Tott's Champagne commercial sotted me with the most beautiful sound and singing. I knew that it was called "aria" because it was Italian and a solo soprano. I hummed the tune for a friend who had been classically trained. "What is that?" I asked in desperation.

"Ah," she said, "You have been captured by Kiri Te Kanawa and "O Mio Babbino" by Puccini.

In my mid-life I have been captured again and again. New age, whatever that meant gave me Enya and "Shepard Moons". Cleveland Chrochet, remember him? Of course not. Cleveland sang Cajun Boogie, a song, called "Sugar Bee". He sang like honey dripping off magnolias, like hot spicy crayfish and rice, like you'll never go home again, "Shugga Be, Shugga Be. It was the first Cajun record to ever hit the Billboard 100. A traveler from Louisiana told me that music is now "Swamp Pop".

My own child singing to her child: "Momma's gonna buy you a mockin bird".

Aretha Franklin in the movie the Blues Brothers, the scene where she sings "Freedom".

The theme from "Out of Africa". Canned Heat and Alan Wilson (Blind Owl) that falsetto pied piper whom I discovered 27 years after Woodstock, "Going Up the Country". Whitney Huston bringing fame to Dolly Parton's "I Will Always Love You". Taylor Swift and Bon Iver's "Exile". Thousands of songs, notes, chords, rhythms, all waiting to be called forth soothing, loving, rousing and remembering.

Postscript: I dislike Rap, no offense to DJ Kool Herc who started this whirl wind in his Sedgewick Ave appartment in the 1970's. The lack of musicality bothered me until I remembered an old blues song from 1926, "Talking Blues" by a fellow named Bouchillon. That song reminded me that Rap is meaning and emotion put to rhythm and has been around a very long time. "If you wanna go to Heaven, let me tell you what to do. You gotta grease your feet in a little mutton stew. Slide right out of the Devil's hand, and ease over in to the Promised Land. Take it easy, go greasy." And Mrs. Kreitler is probably up in Heaven right now, singing "Amazing Grace".

J.L The Tango Dancer

Thigh to thigh, chest to chest, eye to eye,
he became a tango dancer because of a woman.
She spun fine filaments of seduction
until he was enslaved like the Crillo
of the Plate River.
Like them he was slave to that movement of passion,
as the filaments became meshed in his tendons,
snared his mind's neurons, and finally
pierced his pericardium.
All the while he was anesthetized
by the jasmine smell of her skin.
The woman left, but the tango never did.

Reba Owen 01/07/2018

(*Crillo were the Creoles who invented the Tango near the Plate River between Argentina and Uruguay).

The River Forest Gang

We grew up in the Forties, in Oak Grove, Oregon, along the Willamette River. We swam in it polluted, when it was clean, and again when it was in between. We fished crappie, salmon, shad, chubs, and carp. Across the river we snorkeled in Sucker Creek (later euphemised to Oswego Creek). The creek water was clear and green and full of crawfish. My brother got a ten dollar reward for retrieving some guy's glasses.

At night we put a flashlight in a sealed Mason jar and lowered it off the dock in the deeper water of the river to attract catfish to our night crawler bait. We built a campfire on the sand shore. More marshmallows than catfish cutlets ever got eaten by us.

When fog socked in the river, my brother and I would stalk mallards; he with a bow and makeshift arrow, in the front of our row boat, and I at the oars. We would scull quietly within range. No duck ever lost a drop of blood or even a feather at our hands.

The woods were full of old growth oak, firs, and maples in a carpet of trilliums and bracken. Rocky areas held treasures like arrow heads and agates. We found obsidian which we excitedly knew was volcanic. (Actually the black glassy fragments were slag from a turn of the century iron foundry across the river.)

We prayed for flooding in the spring to inundate our homes and streets along the river. I didn't share with my parents that I personally planned to jump off the upstairs balcony and swim around our living room. In winter we wished for a big freeze so our parents could drive down the river to Portland. According to history parts of the Columbia River froze in 1930. However, neither an extreme flood or freeze phenomenon actually happened in our time.

Much of the old neighborhood where the River Forest Gang played is gone. It was replaced by giant homes, six car garages, condos no one could afford, and docks for million dollar boats. Cookie, Dudley, Reba Jo, Trudy, Nancy, Sue, the Mecklem Boys, Larry, Virginia, Claudia, Phil, Billy, Marcia, Linda, the Brown Twins, Gregory, Jeanne, Karen and the youngest John, the first of our gang to go to the Big River in the Sky. He died slowly at his childhood home, the Green House, one of the few original homes left on the street. He left on a golden day in October, as the Willamette flowed by on it's way to the sea.

Defender of the Faith

We were terrified of our new fifth grade teacher at Oak Grove Grade school, 1948. Miss Durkin was about to enter the room. We heard she had been a Catholic school principal. Would she wear a habit? Would she have a pointed stick to tap the maple desks, or worse yet, the heads of misbehavers?

A slender, brown haired, young woman entered and introduced herself. She had eyes a shade lighter than the blue September sky outside. Nothing about her dress (plain skirt and sweater) or demeanor (quiet and kind) caused alarm. If she had a pointed stick it was hidden in her small pocket book.

One of Miss Durkin's first assignments caused my neighbor, Jeanne Kullberg, and I a problem. We were both over-achievers. Miss Durkin assigned a geography exercise as homework.

By 9:00 pm I was in tears. Dorothy Kullberg called my mother to say that Jeanne was sobbing over some assignment the new teacher had given. We were to list all the mountains of the world.

Finally my mother called Miss Durkin at home. "Miss Durkin, sorry to call you so late, but I'm concerned about the home work you assigned. Reba Jo is in tears, and so is our neighbor's child, Jeanne Kullberg. How can you expect them to list all the mountains of the world as an overnight assignment?"

Miss Durkin politely explained that there was a misunderstanding. The assignment was to list the major peaks in Oregon. Since Jeanne and I had already listed all the major rises, hills, extinct volcanos, buttes and peaks both in English names and Indian names, we could go to sleep without dreams of a pointed stick waving in our direction.

So the year progressed, with no more misunderstood assignments. I remember that we made plaster of Paris statues. We poured the mixture in small rubber molds and held them in the sun to dry. No other teacher had ever let us do something as exotic as "plaster of Paris." It was no mystery that our class achievement tests were 2 grades higher that the other fifth grade class.

The most memorable incident happened at Christmas. In 1948, times were less sophisticated. Other children teased Jeanne and I about Santa Claus. We went to Miss Durkin, who we knew, had the answer to all things important. "Is there a Santa Claus?"

"Girls," she said, "Yes of course there is." Those blue eyes looked directly at the teasers. Oh, Jeanne and I believed. We still do today, fifty-six years later.

Reba Jo
10/2006

Fourth of July

As a police detective, our dad had contacts in Portland's Chinatown. Every fourth of July there would be a loud explosion in our yard. I and my siblings leaped from bed, charged outside, and yelled with glee. We then looked all over to see if anything was blown to smithereens. Our dad stood by the garden as if nothing had happened.

During the day we fired off zebras and lady fingers. We lit non-exploding firecrackers called "black snakes" that oozed out a boring squiggle of ash. Sparklers always came with mom's admonition: "Don't poke anyone's eye out or set fire to their hair!"

Occasionally, dad came outside. "Stay back", he would say. He lighted a "red devil". This whirly-gig firecracker spun close to the ground like a small monster looking for toes to shred. The devil left a terror trail of sparks before it blew up at the end.

Even punks were a thing of wonderment. Because the brand name was "camel", we were sure these lighters were made from dromedary dung; dried, odorless dung, pure as far off desert sands.

Our mom cooked. The family barbeque sauce was an all day process. Mom's only other chore was to coax our dog Bobo out of the bathtub after every explosion.

All these activities led to the evening picnic and the non-food items from the Chinese grocery. Roman candles, cherry bombs, more red devils, and whole strings-at-a-time zebras were set off by the adults only. Dad built a wooden ramp for the last event of the evening, sky rockets. The rockets were launched out over the Willamette River. The tail of sparks reflected in a line on the dark surface of the river before the final kaleidoscope blast.

Year after year the fourth was so scripted. In the 1950's civilization came to Oregon. Dangerous fireworks became illegal except in licensed displays. Dad applied and the usual preparations were begun. Unbeknownst to us the local newspaper printed the names and addresses of all the licensees in the state.

About 5:00PM on the fourth, cars started arriving in our neighborhood. People began to wander through our yard to the river bank. Some 200 to 300 jolly people strolled past our red, white, and blue table cloths. They admired the garden. One red-nosed man fell in our little fish pond. Bobo ran howling to the bathtub for good. After that fourth, dad's sky rockets soared and reflected only in our memories.

C Reba Owen 1/1996

Winter Wren Christmas Morning

Drab and cinnamon like dead leaves and dirt.
Shy about the tangled twigs and thicket.
Her quivering throat, the only clue to her disguise.
A winter wren, her song joyous and honeyed.

Who can be sad when she sings?
Who, in agony over wanting those back
who have gone to the soil, cannot be cheered?
Who, though grieving loving words said too late,
would not be soothed by her tremolo?

And who, cannot look forward as her little aria
leads the way to a new dawn on the frost laden forest?

The Greatest Gift

Outside the winter moon reflects in recent rain pools
pools now freezing.
Indoors the oven wafts buttery warmth of spritz and stolen,
blending with the resin air of pine and fir.
Scotch tape and ornament hangers are missing in action
somewhere in the jumble of paper and tissue.
The fire down to rosy coals, the stockings hung there "with care".
Cat "without care" stealing another glass ball off the tree
and batting it under the couch....again.
A choir on PBS singing "O Holy Night",
and my contemplating the greatest gift of all,
being alive.

Reba Owen
12/23/2016

Tables

Mom's table has pills
that don't help,
a vase of lavender
and sage,
and a chord
for oxygen
that won't alter the outcome.
This morning's plate
of small pieces
of mango and nectarine
are there
untouched.

Cookie's table has creme
for skin,
tissues, and a tea
rose by a bible
that won't stop the outcome.
Crumbs from last night's
potato chips
have been brushed
away.

Dad's table has a T.V.
and headphones.
The noise
late into the night
won't change the outcome.
Stockings are there too
in case he has to
rise in the cold
morning hours.

My table has a picture
of handsome parents.
Rays of natural
morning light
illuminate,
but cannot change
their youth.
White lily in an old
purple bottle,
and an empty
moon-snail shell.

Look to your table
before the outcome
cannot be changed,
small stage and
sanctuary
while you slumber
close.

Mors Mortis Morti

When my mother lay bedridden and dying, I tried to cheer her by saying, "Mom you might even live to see the 4th of July." She said, "Honey, don't wish that on me."

Now, at my age I often contemplate death and dying scenarios. When our uncle LG died, people came to the church, but the pastor ushered them past the chapel to the kitchen and community room downstairs. There were donuts and coffee. After thirty minutes the minister began passing out cards which read: "My funeral is now over. Thank you for coming. This card will entitle you to a free tank of gas. Sincerely, LG Mecklem."

Another relative lay dying at the Veteran's Hospital while his very religious niece sat by his bedside. When he began to say, "the light, the light", she, thinking he was seeing a heavenly sign, said, "Uncle shall I call the chaplain?"

The uncle sat right up and said, "Hell no! Close the blinds!"

Other friends and relatives who are still alive have made their wishes known ahead of time. Often the wish to be buried in their favorite place: Uncle Tony in his corn field; friend Trudy under the steps of the Cannon Beach Bakery; my ex on his boogie board and sent out to sea (hopefully after cremation so as not to cause a mess if he washed back to shore).

One summer the whole family took the remains of 2 uncles and 2 aunts to the favorite camping spot on the Deschutes River. We scattered the ashes (a fine white sand) into the clear, snow melt current. I played my ukulele and everyone sang Amazing Grace. Later that day I found an exquisite white rock the size of a swallow's egg. My irreverent cousin said it was just a piece of his mom's ankle bone and that she would have loved for me to have it.

My grand kids think I'm going to live forever. One seven year old told that to his mom. She told him that no one lives forever. The grandson said, "Well, have you looked at her lately?"

This same grandson, now grown, loves a yellow leather couch I have. He was reclining on it one day and asked me to leave it to him. His sister became incensed and chided, "You shouldn't talk like that to gramma."

I said to her, "Isn't there something you want me to leave to you, sweetie?"

"Yes, everything," she answered.

Well, I have told my children that I want to be cremated and scattered in the surf at Falcon Cove (which is probably illegal since it is now a State Marine Reserve). No service, roast marshmallows or something. If they don't do as I wish, I will leave everything to my cats. My daughter always says with a smile, "Well Mom, who do you think will be taking care of those cats?"

"Twilight"

Twilight

Elk are settled in a green pasture by the tree line
where day birds peep their last notes
and a night bird begins his soft song.
A time the poets called "the gloaming".
Twilight years are when we rely on pets
for comfort and companionship when our love
has crossed that line to memory only,
when fear can prevail at each new pain,
or shortened breath. Sounds and sight begin
to blur. Sleep is brief and restless.
When the final twilight comes
one can only hope for a long kind slumber.

Questions for February 14th

On this day think about your greatest love,
is he still there with you, or was he lost long ago
in a whirlwind of words, or a rip tide of regret?
Did he just walk away into an autumn fog on a frosty field?
Or the worst: return draped from some far off desert or jungle?
Perhaps he just met someone else on his way back to you.
Do you remember when you believed he would be there forever,
leaving some purloined lilacs on the kitchen table,
turning the thermostat down after you turned it on high,
putting cream in his coffee?
If your greatest love is still with you, I envy every morning
you get to wake up with your face on his warm back.

Reba Owen 2/14/2021

Tell the Bees

An abnormal February sun has seduced
the Asian pear to bloom early. The winter
heather's perfume tempts bees from their
hive in a hollow alder by the lake.
A Celtic myth says bees are the link to the spirit
world, where all who've passed have gone.
Telling bees is a way to send messages to the
other side, perhaps to those you loved, perhaps
to ones you were not able to tell how much,
before they left..... perhaps you can "tell the bees"
the next time the winter sun warms the purple heather.

R. Owen
6/26/2023

*W*hat Did It Matter?

The bride chose mauve napkins as her accent color
which her future mother-in-law changed to moss green
to lay next to the crystal plates on tables floating on the fake lawn
of the wedding machine Victorian.
Caviar from a slaughtered Beluga sturgeon from the Ukraine,
was served on gluten free crackers shaped like little birds.
The wine was from Cannon Beach
but the wording on the labels said (whispered) "Product of China).
He wanted children, she did not. Perhaps they should have filled out
a questionnaire before the "I do's".
What did it matter the color of the napkins?
What did it matter how many seed pearls were in the bridal costume?
The marriage lasted the requisite seven years and two minutes.
What did it matter how many caviar laden crackers were eaten?
What did any of it matter?

Reba Owen 3/22/22

The Earth Waits

The Christmas lights frame the neighbor children waving sparklers in the dark,
like small clouds of fireflies. In the other dark, the spruce dark another light
peering through as it has for thousands of millennia, unchanged except for
some space debris and human tracks, which only proved the extent of man's indulgence
while the blue earth continues to writhe in pain and foolishness,
spinning and spewing bodies everywhere,
until we survivors are numb and insensitive to the horror of it.
The sparklers are quiet now, the children off to bed.
The moon continues its cold sparkle on the surface of the sea.
Only a silent comber foam breaks the light pattern.
The moon continues, the sea continues, the earth waits.

Reba Owen
12:01 1/1/23

Tony the Carver

He carves images as if the Tlingit, Salish, Haida, and Bella Coola ancestors
had somehow chosen this artist of non-Indigenous origin
to be gifted with their eyes and hands
and 1000 years of knowledge.
These same hands can pick a belle canto
or blues riff with great expertise.
Mask maker, music maker.
Mask maker, jazz man.
Red cedar, bowl maker, song writer.
Like a magician he carved our father's
sea-going dory, after he passed,
into a sleek river craft.
Fisherman, mushroom hunter.

11/8/2023

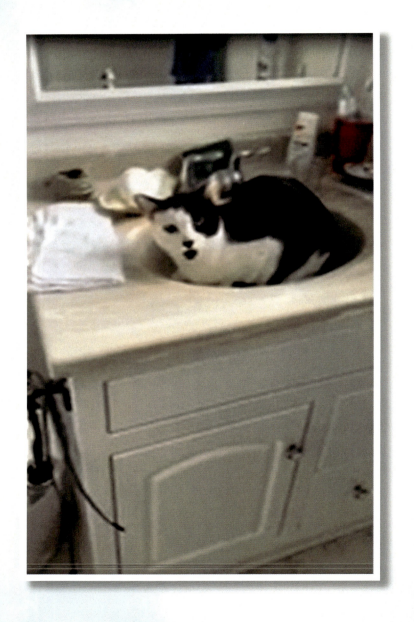

"Let me in"

"You will do as I say" Mochie: You've got to be kidding."

So You Say You Want a Kitten?

So you say you want a kitten? Why not get 2? They can keep each other company. I got two, 8 week old polydactyl cats, brother and sister. They were confined to the office/den until they got over the fear of leaving their mother and other familiar surroundings. They would be indoor pets since coyotes would make short work of them. That meant the dreaded litter box duties for their (or my) life time. The extra toes meant they could scatter more litter around the room. It meant more claws that could get stuck in the curtains as the babies saw who could reach the ceiling the quickest. They also discovered large paddle-shaped paws are great for splashing liquids out of the water dish onto the floor.

But, back to the litter box. All the products say "odor free". Well it is a big lie! In order to mask any noxious smells I burned a pine scented, votive candle on my desk, my desk where I worked at my computer. "How did this happen?" the computer repair guy asked. He said he had cleaned many exotic coffee drinks out of a key board, but never any pine scented wax. "Oh I picked up the votive candle, the glass was hot, I have cats, well it is a long story." For an extra $34 he did a rush cleaning.

The baby shots and cat toddler, well- baby exams at the vet came to $80 each. New curtains, $89, (not only did they hang from their claws, but the little girl got her teeth stuck and was hanging one time). Who knew that kittens could get up on a refrigerator and knock a vase of flowers off of it? (Multiple times.)

Their release to the wider jungle of living room, baths, kitchen would provide new adventures: throwing up food they didn't like, hair balls, playing in the toilet and thousands of new places to attempt claw sharpening even though they have an expensive scratching post $45. After a washer repair (the drain was clogged with some kind of animal hair), I realized that all dirty clothes had to be air fluffed in the drier before washing.

On the plus side, they purr and act like you are their mother. Oh, and they sleep a lot! Up to 17 hours but not necessarily at night. At night they will often scratch on your bedroom door and meow loudly to see if you are alright.

Carey's Customers

My sister-in-law worked at the First Interstate Bank at the drive through window. She became quite fond of certain customers . They came in regularly with their owners. The bank would go through a large sack of dog biscuits two times a month. There was a big black lab named "Fred "who sat on the passenger side very politely and calmly. He ate the treat with proper manners. Some of the smaller dogs like "Killer" and "Peaches" would go into a frenzy as soon as their owners got up to the service window. They would jump over the seats, whirl around and yap incessantly till the treat was offered.

Several owners say their dogs developed language skills around their trips to the B_A_N_K! Just the mention of those four letters would cause them yip excitedly, cock their ears, or run toward the door or the garage.

No one ever brought a cat to the drive through. It is probably a Class C Driving offense to have a cat loose in a moving vehicle.

Carey & Dudley Cove Beach Sunset

Disappearing Brownie Blues

I went to the cupboard, the brownies were gone
don't know how much weight I've put on.
I've got the blues, I've got the blues
I've got the disappearing brownies, disappearing brownie blues.

This pandemic is getting me low,
don't know how much longer I can go,
I got the blues, I got the blues,
I've got the disappearing brownie, the disappearing brownie blues.

The pan was empty, the pan was bare,
Got more inches on my deiriere.
I got the blues. I've got the blues
I've got the disappearing brownie, the disappearing brownie blues.

Woke up this morning, went to the store
All my clothes don't fit anymore.
I got the blues, I got the blues
I got the disappearing brownie, the disappearing brownie blues.

Empty brownie pan

The Shadow

Fear is the shadow in the shrubbery
that even bright moonlight cannot define.
It is a dark pattern beyond a gray wave,
under spreading foam that distorts seal or shark?
Fear is a shadow on an x-ray when a cough is bloody.
But fear also is a feeling that rides love.
The chance that love will disappear
or change, or be ripped away in a sudden unfair event.
Fear is always in our lives somewhere,
waiting when we are tired or our guard is down,
especially at night, in dreams,
when it is quiet and that wraith wakes you
with his creaking steps.
As you lie there, try to think about noonday
when the honeysuckle is warm in the sun,
and fear is sleeping,

Reba Owen
11/01/2020

"Moon Dog"

Sailor's Warning

Looking to the east the sky is a sailor's warning.
I am swaying from the stupor of a night
dreaming of you.
We are together again in that musty cottage
hidden in the trees.
Years of anger and tears staining the walls.
The years of broken egg shells scattered about.
In the dream I know I have a new place
unbeknownst to you, and my cats are unfed, and
I can't remember the address.
Part of me knows I can awake and you'll evaporate.
It's as if I am sedated and split in two. You leave, but
the door is locked You are hiding on the other side
to see if I lose my senses. I wake.
Out the window the red sky reflects in the lake,
foretelling a soft rain that is about to happen. The cats
are snuggled next to me.   11/4/2023

New Years

The rising winter moon has turned the alder bones to frost.
(In the morning there will be a skin of ice on the lake).
I try to remember how many times you kissed me at midnight
on a New Years Eve.
I can only remember one. Because it was the same full moon,
but rising over spruce and hemlock.
You came home in time to hold me tight,
with the quiet sound of the surf behind us.
If I dreamed of you again after all these years,
Your walk would be the same, but not your face. I can't reach it anymore.
It seems those convoluted white, alders are a mirror of neurons,
so tangled, that all warm memories of New Years are now frozen hard,
and fractured forever.

Segrid's Blues

A
Blue coffee, blue tea,
D   A
Blue coffee blue tea
E7   A7
Everything I drink tastes blue to me.

A
Ever since you cut me free,
D   A
Ever since you cut me free,
D   A
Every kiss feels blue to me.

A
Every song I sing seems so,
D   A
Every song I sing seems so,
E7   A
Different shades of indigo.

A
Blue coffee, blue tea,
D   A
in my mind and memory,
E7   A
Your sky eyes they torture me.

Reba Owen
9/30/2022

The News

Morning light has turned the mud flats to silver.
White pelicans are splashing there
as if tumbled pieces from the cumulus thunderheads.
The salmon who passed there in the moonlight
are upstream now, making redds in the gravel
under the shelter of willow branches.
Who can be fearful in such a scene?
Even the thunderheads are silent.
The lightening will sleep until the next cold front
collides with the southern wind.
Still there is a feeling of anxiety, ominous and even with eyes closed
sinuous pictures appear: wounded children, burned vehicles and worse.
Lies, deceit, face book prophets saying "the apocalypse is near; and there
is nothing we can do about it."
Ah, but there is....
tomorrow I will take my computer and TV to Goodwill.

Reba Owen
11/08/2019

Woolly Bear

A woolly bear is on the beach
far from sustenance and cover,
exposed to crows and combers.
It knows nothing of lemmings.
It knows nothing of fame in forecasting winter.
The woolly bear has tiny eyes, so tiny
perhaps she took a wrong turn
to end up on this Sahara of sand.
Or as my friend, Pam, opined,
the woolly bear was suicidal over 2020.
She now recuperates in her savior's garden.

Hornet's Nest in the Heather

A hornet's nest is in the heather,
marked by a swirl.
They feed on nearby fallen pears, each wasp
taking a sugar offering back to the queen.
There is an urgency to their working
Because......
soon they will lie still in the dew.
A hornet's nest is in the heather,
and I wonder if there is meaning
in the rhythm and tempo of the autumn.
It would seem things rush to finish,
to ripen, to burst shells and husks.
A harvest of memories blows on the cooling breeze.
Candied apples, leaf smoke, fright at a new grade school teacher
the mystery of how fog rises from a field,
or spruce shadows forming from a hunter's moon.
A hornet's nest is in the heather,
where frost and silence will cover there soon.

Reba Owen
10/24/2020

Nocturne

Curtains of snow appear
from the heavy
atmosphere
to bend leaves still left
and fill the v's
of branches.
Even in this soundless
drift, the
owl can sift
feet and tails
as warm things
push their
grainery trails
beneath the
white whispers.

Uber

Today I saved a baby
crab spider, smaller than a peppercorn,
a creamy yellow newborn.
He was, as if by magic, hanging to the steep precipice
of my Toyota truck door.
I presented him with a fluffy daffodil
which he quickly embraced and disappeared
into the golden depths.
It seemed a puzzle what morsel would be
small enough for him to eat.
To ensure his survival from the destined-to-wilt flower,
I gave him a free uber ride to a live, butter colored primrose plant.

Reba Owen
5/3/2023

*D*rought

Drought, thirty seven days without,
in a place known for rain.
Yes, some virga in the early morning,
no sign left by nine.
The town hall lawn is green, though
and crows are bathing in the sprinklers.
Smart birds. They fluff their feathers, and hop about.
Ponds have dried so mosquitos are almost gone.
Violet green swallows feed their young on the last swarms.
Sunsets are epic, fed by southern wildfire smoke
hundreds of miles away.
Drought in rain land.
The crows are trying to find the sprinkler
on/off switch.

Reba Owen
8/01/2021

Photosynthesis

it
is
the
map
of three
seasons a
sap stream
of sugar, carbon
and water, tempting
teeth and beak, of hoof and
wing bright green in spring but
red and brown by fall sometimes
yellow, bug ravaged, destined to soil
poplar, birch, willows, ginko apple
oak maple holly walnut pear
peach, alder, plum, fir
cottonwood
cypress
l
e
a
v
e
s

ou

I always thought I would see you again
digging clams on a fall-swept beach,
sun going down, October moon rising from the dunes.
I always thought you'd be there
where we made love along a green steelhead stream,
on a yellow bed of maple leaves,
while overhead pairs of geese were heading south.
I look for you, with time running out,
because I always thought I'd see you again.

10/24/2020

$\mathcal{D}$uet the Owl

I can ripple the moon
and scatter the stars
on the surface of the lake
at night.
I can duet the owl
and the soaring
night hawk,
but I am helpless
to ever find you again.

R Owen 6/8/2023
copyright

Reba Owen is Northwest Oregon poet, artist, and blues player. She is a graduate of Oregon State University with a major in Recreation. This third book is about many memories from her youth and poems that celebrate our beautiful paradise here on the Oregon coast. As in past books she used nature to sometimes expose the foibles of humans and their activities. The world wide situation right now as we know is difficult and alarming. Hopefully this book will be a diversion for a short time for the reader. A noctilucent cloud is very rare. The author has seen one only twice and is grateful to have witnessed that phenomenon. Observing nature is one small way to find peace and sense at times.

11/09/2023

Printed in the United States
by Baker & Taylor Publisher Services